Book 2

PATHWAYS

Ian Hibburt

Cover design: Busybird Publishing

Layout and typesetting: Busybird Publishing

Busybird Publishing
2/118 Para Road
Montmorency, Victoria
Australia 3094

www.busybird.com.au

I dedicate this book to all my special friends
And to Dianne, my soul-mate and inspiration.
Also the others who have helped.

Special thanks to Margaret, Ruth, Sarah and Mel and Nancy
For all their encouragement and understanding

Contents

Chapter 1

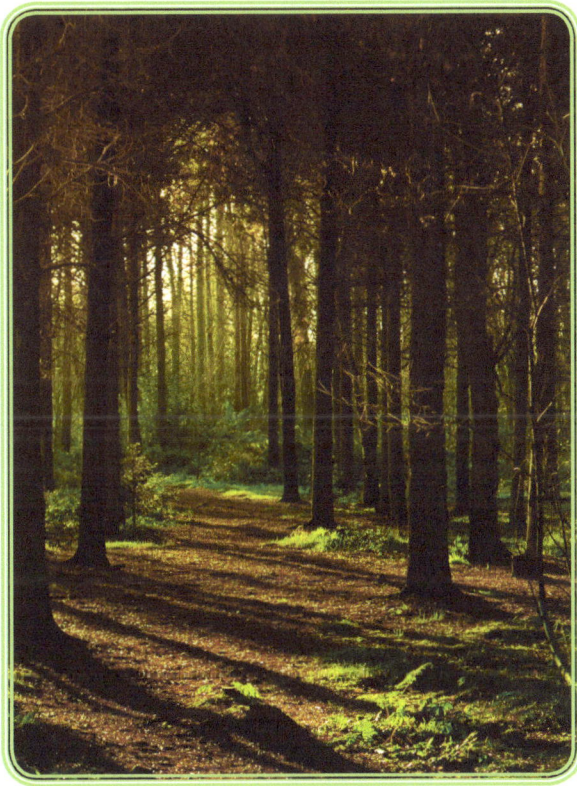

Pathways

Pathways

I am walking beneath ancient trees
Sunlight on grass
An emerald glow
Toadstools making poisoned chalices
Among the shadows
Following the pathway
To where? I don't know-
The Journey is here
To be made-
Experiences and truths to discover-
Pathways to tread.

Forest Pathway

Not a sound is heard.
Mist silently curls and slides
Over the boughs and branches
Of the old trees.
They have seen many summers
And also the coldness of winters embrace;
Counting through the years, through the seasons
A young breeze playfully swirls the fog
Around the ancient trunks and the mist
Clears to reveal the arched canopy of trees
Stretching to the sky over the
Pathway through the forest.

This is a magical place and the others are here:-
Refugees from the past
With the memories

That refuse to die.
They remember the good times when
Man and nature
Worked together in harmony
Times of peace and plenty
And they lament the progress of greed
Across the land
Warning us to stop
Before it's too late.
And we talk and I tell them they are heard
And remembered.
Some still care
Some still appreciate
The beauty of the earth.

Finding Gia

Easily he slipped into the saddle
And turning to wave, gave a shout
And rode out into the setting sun.

He's gone a-wandering
Following the wanderlust
And the min min lights
Out onto the plains of grass and clay.
Down the trails made by Kangaroos
Tracks to the water hole
And up the steep rise
Here he pauses,
To gaze at the dying embers
Of the sunset

Soon he will make camp
Under some spreading gum tree
A fire and billy tea.

Laying on the warm sand
Quietly watching, as the stars light up the sky
So quiet he can hear the earth breathing,
The ebb and flow, rise and fall
That special energy that fills us all

It's in the solitude of the bush
That he hears the rhythm of earth
And feels the pulse of Gia.

Past midnight and
The moon has risen
Faintly, in the distance
Dingos howl.

The Beach

Over the hill and down cutty grass track
Along by the creek till the bush gives way
To sand hills of black sand.

The long graceful crescent of the beach stretches
Till it ends at the cliffs
Waves rush to the beach
To collapse in lacy foam.

A solitary Albatross
Gracefully floats in the air
Riding the winds with ease.
How far has he flown
To be here today
At the beach?

Oak Trees

My ancestors lived amongst
Oak forests in England
So when I see a massive
Tree like this
It triggers deep
Memories in my soul
A feeling of belonging to a distant past.
That's what looking up into this tree
Means to me, connection;
To my past memories.

Kilmore Creek

The creek has a secret life
Hidden among the rushes
Are the insects, animals and birds
That live here
Trees crowd the banks
Seeking water
This is a magical place
Where fish swim
In the dark waters.

And it has it's seasons
Drought when it nearly dies
And flood when it
Rages down the valley,
And the quiet times
In between.

Purest Blue

When the sky is the purest blue
And the sunlight sparkles
On every leaf and flower
Joy fills my heart
And Love soothes my soul

The world is at peace
And the birds sing opera
In the trees.
We glimpse the paradise
Surrounding us with wonder

And we are happy
Loving each other
And being here today

The Old Church

The old church on the hill is empty now
Windows barred, stained glass enmeshed
For protection.

This symbol of eternal life now abandoned.
Built in more optimistic times
When faith and hope were needed
To survive the harsh life of pioneer days.

People have moved to the city
In pursuit of fortune and fame,
Sinners all of them.
Only the stone church remains—
Cold and hard as the protestant forefathers.

The Chimney

A chimney still stands.
That's all that's left of the lives
That were here.
Yes there were good times, happy times,
And a good harvest.
Then the drought came
And everything died
Dreams into dust
All that's left is
A chimney
That stands, alone.

The Secret Track

Hidden among the ferns and bushes
Is the entrance to my secret track.
Discovered by accident while looking for
A way down from the cliffs
Of the Maori look-out.

The Manukau harbour glistens
In the morning sun—
A rising spring tide

The track winds its way down past
The sugarloaf— a good fishing spot,
But, I'm following the track further
To where it ends at the small beach
Under the cliffs.

Hanging onto the sandstone rock-face
Like some crazy climber
A Pohutukawa tree canter-levers
Over the water.
White shelly sand lines the small
Crescent of the beach,
And assorted detritus lies jumbled
Along the high tide line.

I have come here to fish for Piper,
But, I really have come here,
To be one with nature.

Chapter 2

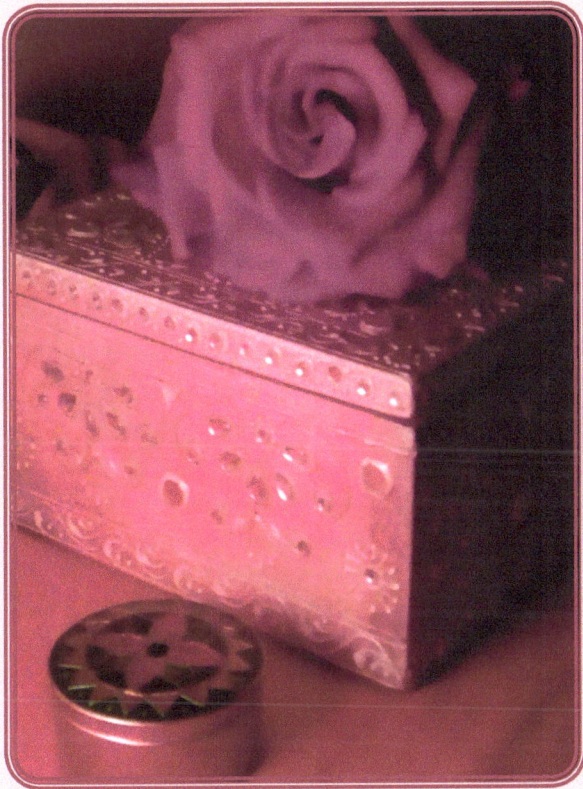

Love

Broken Heart

A heart was broken
All those years ago
Love that was to last a life time
Betrayed and broken
When hurtful words were spoken
So deep was the hurt—
Never spoken of again,
There in the shadows.
When in time, in years,
Life was reborn
Love dried your tears,
And healed your fears
And now you walk down the path
Of goodness and light
Where everything that's wrong
Is made right.
There is no night
There is no pain
There is no sadness
Only light and gladness.

Our Love

Everything has changed since we fell in Love
The world is a brighter place, smiles upon our faces
Living in the joy of loving each other
To Love and be Loved in return
Is the greatest gift you could ever earn.
She gives to me the Love I need
And I Love her with all my soul.
To be entwined in the energy of pure Love
Is to become one with each other and with God
Completeness fills my soul
And we are living on the edge of eternity.
Love is eternal.

Love is my drug

Love is my drug
And I am so high
I may never come down
I could stay like this forever
Love is the drug I seek
Love makes me complete.
7/5/19

Love's destiny

We were destined to meet
At this point in time
Our Love waiting to be born
Within our arms to fill our longings
And heal our sorrow
We are made for each other
And the sweetness of our Love
Cannot be described—
Ah the crushing desire of wanting you
With all my heart
And the joy of feeling your love
It is all too much!
Can you die from too much Loving?
No, Love, it cuts you, then it heals you
To experience Love in all its fullness
Nearly kills you
Then it heals you and you are reborn
A different person transformed
by the purity of true Love
an everlasting diamond.

Never to be apart

Two o'clock in the morning
And I am missing you
I want to feel you
Laying here beside me,
Your breathing
Quietly soothing my soul
Your Love making me whole.

And tomorrow it begins
Our life together
Engulfing each other
In the vastness of our Love

Love so delicate; elegant and sweet
Love so deep and strong.
With each other is where we belong—
Never to be apart.

Angel's Wings

Just to know that you are there
And how much you care
Gives me the strength to carry on

"Your love touches me
Gentle as Angels wings"

And speaks to me
Deep in my heart
The secrets of my Love are yours
And we are together again.

Great Love

Great Love is a rare and precious thing
Never let it fade away and die.

Each kind word and act of Love
Stokes the flame of passion

Never forget how lonely we were
Before we met.
Never forget the joy that filled our soul
And the Love that made us whole.

They say that Love is blind
Yes it is—blind to all those little faults
We still have:- but Love sees into our heart
And fills it with it's warm glow.

Kaleidescope

My
Heart is
Full of hope
Sadness and joy
Life in me
Flowing, flowing
Deeper and deeper
Down the river of
Life, stronger
And stronger
Each day.

A Rose—joy
A thorn—sorrow
I choose to feel the pain
So I can feel the joy.
Pain will fade away
To be replaced with
Pleasure
We are moving through a
Kaleidescope of emotions,
On and on…

The Lovers

Under the twinkling stars
The lovers walked
Down by the lake
Through the velvet darkness
Of the shadows
And their bodies touched
In warm embrace
Spirits and hearts entwined
Waves lapped quietly at the beach
Eternal Love and Earthly Love meet
Together in that magical moment in time
And they are transformed
Within the energy of pure Love.

Love's Crying

Love's crying in the dark
For its lost children—
Who have turned away from
Freedom and truth
And gone a wandering into
The forests of fantasy, deception and lies.
To follow the never-ending promises
Of success and fame
To chase the mirage of happiness
In possessions that they buy.

One day the sun will shine
And the mists will clear
And Love's truth will lead
Them home along that
Golden shining path.

Welcome home my children,
Welcome back into the light
Of my Love.

Chapter 3

Encouragement

Easy / Hard

I used to say, this is easy, this is hard.
I can do this, I can't do that
I have the skills for that
I have no skills for this
What a silly thing to do
Decide in advance what
I can and can't do!
This is wrong.
This attitude I must change
Shut down those thoughts of doom
Shut up the "Nark"
I am doing this today
I will let myself do it
Slowly working through it.
No more self-sabotage
This is easy not hard!

Land of too hard

The fields of achievement lay fallow
In my land of too hard.
I am guilty of neglecting
Parts of my life which
I thought were too hard to fix
Too hard to live
The problem unsolvable.

These fields of weeds and neglect
Can become the perfect opportunity
To reclaim my life in its entirety
Are you brave enough
To be the man to make this happen?
Yes! I will be brave
I will make this work
It's not the way I thought it would be- it never is
Walk over the bridge
And through the door
Into a different reality.

I can't do this!

I can't do this, I feel over-whelmed
I feel weak and scared.

What's this I can't?
You can and you will!
No time for regrets
No time for fears
No time for second thoughts
No—
We are doing this!
Hang on for the ride
Get on side
The roller coaster's
About to leave.

Outside the Comfort Zone again.
Hit "fast forward" if you dare!
You will never be left wondering "what if"?
You will never be bored or unhappy'
Your life will never be the same
Follow your heart and fly like the Eagle
Into God's sky.
Trust the one above who gives his love
You can do this!

Lost Opportunities

When I think of all the lost opportunities
That I have had, it makes me sad
Yes- even regret

Looking back from here
Knowing what I know now
I can see how different my life would be,
If I'd chosen differently.

It's easy to see from here what I should've done
But, this is non-sense because
I did not know, what I know now

A little bit of should have,
Could have, if only
Why didn't someone tell me?
How silly was I? Why did I do that?

Well I did what I thought was the right thing at that time
Of course I didn't know, what I know now.
Clear the decks. Start over!
What's done is done
Good, bad and ugly
This is the result of my decision

No more recrimination
No more guilt
No more self-flagellation
No more victim
No more pain

Assets and liabilities that's all
That's my starting point
What's all this emotional pain
attached to this? This angst?

Time for the cleansing,
Time to choose some good memories
To cling to, time to make the bad stuff
Disappear from memory
Into the sea of forgetfulness.
Time to release all that energy
That's tied up in regret, guilt and angst.
Time to let it all go.

When that's done we start fresh
In the sun
We have Hope
That this can be undone
None of this will be a problem—
But, an opportunity
To put my new skills to work.

Don't look back

The moment of knowing
When all the energy of Love and pain and desire
And the experiences of life are felt
Like a huge storm of memories.

I must give thanks for every experience
And let it go,
Let it die
That I might
Be reborn
Let it go,
Walk away,
No regrets,
Don't look back.
Free the energies
Tied up in the past
Let them fly, like Doves into the sun
Let it return to you
Let it be your new strength
To be that new person.

The Choice

The ship tied up in port is safe and secure
It will never face the storm. It will never be damaged,
Or sink in the deep.
To experience the thrill of being alive,
The wind in our hair,
We must cast off without a care
Follow the compass over the far horizon
Into the land where everything is dangerous
But, Awesome.

The pain of too much love
Joy without limits
The splendour of life
Unfolding in all its terror and extreme
Explosion of life in all its forms.
Choose your life.

Walk away

Walk away…
Never go back.
Escape the prison
Made of rules and fear

Walk away…..
Never return here
Be free like you
Are meant to be.

Walk away…..
Do not miss
The security of the rules
Remember the guilt and fear
And pain they caused.

Walk away…..
Leave this world
Of rules and judgement
Be free to live again.
Walk away…..

Walk into the sun
Leave the shadow world
Where people are only
Half alive.

Step through the door
Into freedom
Here is a whole new
World to live in
Peace and Love are here.

A new life
With no limits
A new life
With nothing holding
Me back.

Yellow Rose

Against the darkened room
A yellow rose glows
In the transient
Autumn sun light

And joy rises in my soul
As this flower of beauty
Awakens sleeping emotions
Reminding me that
Life is still worth living

Even if we are locked down
And freedom is the first casualty
Of the virus.

Beauty

The beauty of this world
So casual and perfect
Take time to admire
The creator's work
And give thanks for all the good things
In life.

Finding Joy

I can find joy in a rock ballad,
And sweet empathy with Pie Jesu
And be filled with Love
Listening to adagio
Or feel like dancing with Patricia Kass
Singing chante le blues
Also
I can rejoice in the shape and space
Of a Henry Moore sculpture
Or admire the cool elegance of a
Pounamu jade carving,
Experience the beach boulder
Heavy in my hand,
Feel the sand beneath my feet
And listen to the distant roar
Of the surf pounding the beach
And then the tinkling of a stream
Returning to the sea from which it was born.

I hear the Bell Bird and the Tui
Singing in the damp bush
As the fish swim silently up stream,
Cool playful breezes tug at my hat and
The sun stretches my shadow
Across the pebbly bank.
I can return to my studio
And create delicious harmonies
In colour across the canvas
Colours so vibrant and alive
Like a symphony played in the open air
YES life is good—
So much beauty
So much joy.

End of the day

The dramas of today
Are washed away into
The sea of forgetfulness

Happy Loving thoughts
Caress my mind
Creating harmony.

Chapter 4

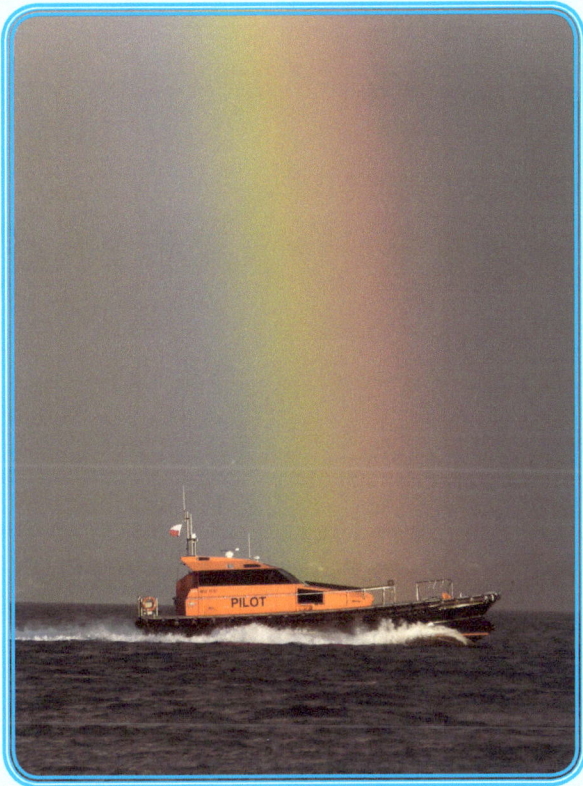

Guidance

The Angel speaks

Suddenly I am aware
That I am not alone
He has come to speak
To tell me about what I seek.

The Angel speaks
But not in words-
They could not convey
What he has to say.

Visions of space without dimension
Inspiring thoughts and feelings and power
Burning in my soul, energy to make me whole
Healing fullness complete-
Mere words cannot covey
What my Angel has to say.

Elephant In The Room

How long can you ignore me?
While I'm standing here in your room?

I'm standing here to remind you
Of something that you forgot.
I'm not here to recall a debt or guilty sin,
No! nothing like that!

I've been collecting all those dreams you gave up on.
All those creative projects you were inspired to do
But life and circumstances prevented you.

This is a new spring
And broken dreams can be healed
So retrieve those visions
And be inspired again
Breath life back into your dreams
And take time to live again.
Go back to the age of innocence

When you saw the blue sky
And felt the warmth of the sun
Even the stars were within your grasp

Go back to before your life was crushed
Under the heavy weight of sin and obligation
And you became imprisoned by self-doubt.

Walk away—be free
Step into a new life of freedom and happiness
Focus on the positive
And forget all that negative stuff—
You don't need it anymore.

So having said his message
My big grey elephant slowly dematerialises
His last words
" REMEMBER THIS"

Jumbo's Back

Hello Jumbo—you're back I see
Yes, there's something else
I want to say—
You will be surprised by JOY
And confronted with SADNESS
But they are emotions
We feel—
You cannot grasp the wind
In your hand.
We are moved by the wind
As it breaths through us
This is the flow of life,
Like a melody going on and on
Sometimes repeating
As we join in the
Song of the universe.

Angel of Mercy

The Angel of mercy came to me
And said "Don't be so hard on your-self,
You are chucking down your life
By being so hard on your-self—
Should, shouldn't must, mustn't
That's no good! You aren't good at that.
Wait-up Son; who said
You had to be perfect first time,
Anytime. Why rush to judge
Something a failure.
Don't be hard
Don't hate your-self
How about a bit of love
For your-self.
You're okay loving others,
You're okay showing others mercy
And consideration
Now it's time for you."

Meditating

I gaze into the pool
Of crystal clear water

Dark shapes flit to and fro
Quietude in my soul
My mind rests
And thoughts
Come and go
The surface is smooth
As liquid silver
Above conscious
Below, my deepest thoughts

I summon him from
The depths below
Where he sleeps
Oblivious of the
Drama and turmoil above

Faintly the dark form
Materialises into focus,
A giant turtle rises to the surface
He is old, old as time itself.

"Hello son," he says
"What's happening?"
I tell him and he says
"Oh that old thing again!"
"So you know about this?"
I say amazed.
I think this situation is unsolvable!,
A blind alley, a dead end.

"No!" he laughs "That's what you think ,
So that's what you've got!
"I don't think that at all."
Now here's what you do,
And he tells me the simple way
To change my thoughts—
Change my reality.

Ah, he begins to sing,
You are a young one,
Love life and life will love you,
Let your thoughts make wings
And fly up high—
Be free, be happy
Be at one with the universe—
Don't fight it.

And with that he slowly
Began to sink deeper, deeper
Till he vanished from sight.

Moving On

I am moving on,
Going forward into the new.
But, my friends are concerned
Wait, look what you have left behind!

The book of rules you must obey—
Just thrown away!
And won't you need your precious possessions
Won't you need any of your old life?

Only the memories of my dear wife
Will I need. The rest I'm letting go
Because I'm moving on
But always keeping her
Love in my heart.

Nadir

Ground zero
Flash of light
Karmic debt repaid
Nothing then something
Act of creation
Genesis
New beginning
Reality changes
As I do.

Lying here

Lying here in bed
Silently watching the
Thoughts flowing
Through my head.

Runes telling me to take care—
Disruption is coming
Into my life

Runes telling me of
Strength and resolve
Also of care and patience
Required; progress to be made.

Thoughts of unfettered joy
And happiness have dissolved
Into nothingness.
Where did they go?

The Blind Man

A blind man met an Angel
Who was giving away special glasses
That would restore sight to the wearer
Take these the Angel said,
These glasses will make
You see and they are free!

"What use are they to me" he said
"Can't you see that I'm blind".

"Indeed you are!"
The Angel said.

Chameleon

I am something else
What have I become?
Changing, changing
With the landscape
Of some foreign dream
Changing like some
Multi-coloured Chameleon
Just when you think you know me
I go to another level
Another place

I am exploring the taboo truths
I am breathing the air of strange philosophies
I am experiencing the new, the old, the strange
The odd.

Out there the truth is waiting to reveal it's self to me
I can play hide and seek till the cows come home
I can move unseen against the pattern of life
But, she can find me
Just like that!
She sees through my disguise
She looks into my eyes
And I cannot hide
She looks into my eyes
And sees my heart
She sees and knows the real me
And she loves me for who I am.

Valley of Tears

Life is a journey and I am lost
In the valley of tears

I am held here by my fears
And I must stay until I find a way
To give these tears away

Crying from the depths of my soul
The pain that will not heal
Feeling so sad that
My Love has gone
Can I ever live and Love again?

One day I will reach the end of this valley of tears
One day I will climb the mountain of happiness again.
One day I will feel no more pain.
One day the grief will be gone—
And I will be reborn.

Chapter 5

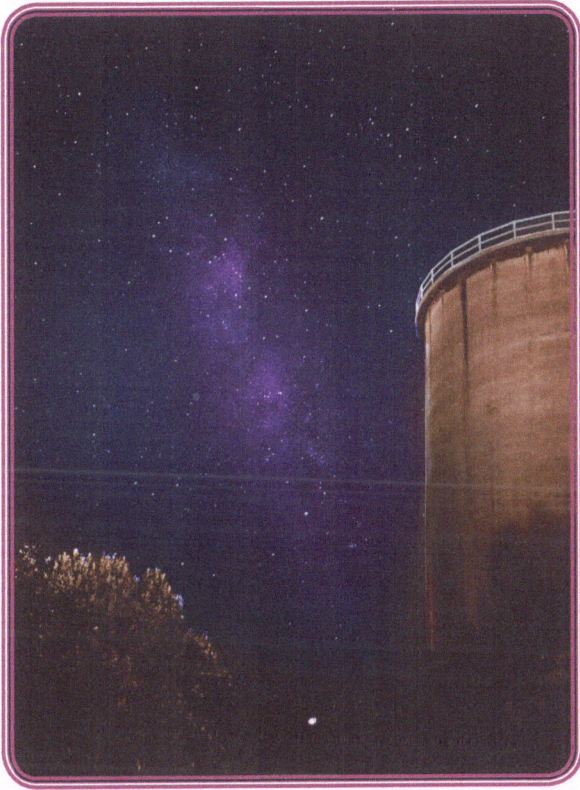

"Out There"

The Paradox of God

He is so big it's unimaginable
Yet he is within each
Particle of energy and life
He is vaster than the universe
But he is here with me
To chat about my cares and fears
And he does not "fix" anything for me;
Wave a magic wand. No he makes a way
For us to grow and learn as we sort
Our own problems out—
Sure he will send help, but lets us achieve
For ourselves.

Being Me

The sun was shining
The air was clear
I am standing tall
Sky of blue
Grass so green
The sheep are there:-
Just being sheep
I am here:-
Just being me.
Standing before God
In his world of beauty
I feel no fear or humility
No guilt or shame
I am me
A human doing human things
As I was created to be
I am complete-content
And God approves,
I am okay.

Never the same

Your life will never be the same, they said.
And they were right.
Moving in the flow—
Letting cares and worries go
Taken by Love to the world above
And through eternity's gate
Into that land of love and light
Where everything is changed
Such Joy and bliss
I never knew life could be like this
I could go on into eternity
And never return
But I must go back
With my heart full of happiness
And bring eternity to earth.

Dying

The final cold embrace
Sucks my life away
Falling helpless into the grave
I am gone, done, finished.
This is the end I feared.

Dark velvet night
Invades my soul
As I walk the pathways
Of the night.

So this is it,-death
I was expecting sharp and painful
But this is like a candle going out.

Come said the voice
They are waiting for you
A vast land of light and energy
And people, so many people
This is the after-life.

Night Revelation

I had a dream—
Everyone else was asleep
I was woken by the presence of an Angel
"Come outside and look at this" he said.
So I went outside and looked up into the clear night sky.
And wonders did I behold,
Space was there in all its infinite glory
And the spiritual Beings, full of light,
Emotion and knowledge made themselves known
Then drifted out of sight.
Angels came and went on their missions
And more, much more
An overwhelming revelation
Of the higher worlds out there—
Just beyond our normal sight
I am buzzing with energy.
I went inside to tell them—
But they were all asleep.
Wake up people! There's more to life
Than the physical world we see.

Mi Mi Beach

The night was very quiet
The distant drum of surf pounding
On the beach
Drifted in through the window
Somewhere in the house
I could hear the rattling of a mouse

Then all quiet—
Memories of the old people
Wound their way into my mind-
Reminding me of lives once lived,
And battles fought and lost
Of victory and tragedy
All those deep and dark emotions
Which refuse to die.
I hear you my friends
The old ones who remain
Afraid to go on and be forgotten

I feel your pain—
But can't you forgive your enemies
And let yourself travel on to Waikiki
And there be at peace?

After some time
There is movement
And they are moving
Out up the hill and over there
To the land of the spirits of the dead.

All is quiet now--
Very quiet
Even the mouse has gone to bed
The surf drums in the distance

Blue Light Portal

Through the portal of blue light
Down the path of peace and harmony,
I travel leaving baggage behind me
Cares and worries drop away
Like falling leaves
And I bare my soul to the healers
Who, with Love and Grace
Surround my life with
Healing thoughts and feelings.
Letting go and moving in the flow
I float into the healing power of God's Blue Light
Impossible, eternal creatures live here.
They are curious to meet this traveller
Through space and time, brought
From Earth's existence.
We look into each other's eyes
And communicate
The deep memories of our souls.
Now they understand grief and pain.
Now I understand light and power
Our lives have interleaved
For a moment in time
And now we return
To our separate worlds.

Nexus

Sometimes the unexpected happens
And this road I'm travelling
Intersects with a different reality
And for a while the physical
And the eternal co-mingle
The nexus where miracles occur
And access to other worlds is easy.

That place of peace and harmony
Elegance and beauty
And I am there, just being free
Being me.
And I am flying to that far horizon
Where all dreams are possible
And reality bends into a new existence.
No going back, even if you wanted to.
Wow.

Fast forward

Sometimes events conspire
To confront me with the issues
That will not go away.

Demanding my attention,
A lesson to be learned
Truth that requires change
As proof of its reality

Hagiliz; disruption; awakening.
Pain followed by joy

The old must be processed/sorted
Before the new can burst forth and grow.

Why do we fear change
Things that won't change
Become fossils—
Turned to stone like Goblins
Caught in the sun's rays.

We all know people
Caught in a time warp
Repeating the same patterns
Over and over like some stuck record—
Until it's impossible to change
Their safe routines have become a prison
With bars stronger than steel.
Instead we should fear a life stuck
On pause/repeat.
If you are brave enough hit "PLAY"
Even "FAST FORWARD" if you dare
And I promise you, your life
will never be the same!

YEE HAH!!

The Ancient Ones

Nothing moves
All is quiet
Stillness reigns
Rocks sleep
Beside the dark
River pools.
The waning moon
Reflects it's mellow
Light across the still water

Ancient ones are
Camping by a dying fire
Its smoke rises
Straight up
Forming a pillar
Between heaven and earth.

Chapter 6

Animals and Others

Three Birds Flying

Today I saw three birds flying
White feathers on a blue sky
Moving together towards their goal
Freedom, happiness on the wind.

To me they mean
Freedom and happiness
And when I see them
My heart is lifted with joy

Fly on to that far horizon
Where all your dreams come true!

Ibis are flying today

The Ibis are flying today
White wings against
A grey sky
Flying in formation
All with one mind
Heading south to feed
In the swamp of reeds

Ibis are flying
They sing to me of freedom
And places faraway
They are one with the sky
And each other.
Disappearing from sight
To the land beyond.

The Egret—(Patience)

The Egret has infinite patience
Wading precisely through the shallows
Seeking out its unwary prey.

The Egret believes that this
Is the right hunting ground for him
And with faith and patience he will succeed.

I think these qualities are hard-wired into the Egret's brain.
We would give up after 15 minutes
And fly away seeking better hunting grounds
And so on through the day
Till we give up having caught nothing.
Yes, we can learn a lot from the Egret.

Poem of The Lone Wolf

Lone Wolf looks at me,
Pale eyes the colour of ice
She has been patrolling
The paths of the night
Under the pale moon.
She speaks to me of the
Mysteries of the mountains
Of ice and snow, and the
Secrets of the dark forest.
She is strong; she is free and wild.
My Lone Wolf from the lands beyond.
Sings to the moon and is gone.

The Lone Wolf Returns

The Lone Wolf, has returned
She looks at me
Eyes the colour of blue ice
And at her feet
Three pups happily play,
Full of bright energy
And fight.
In the distance I see him, her mate
Strong and fierce
Her protector.
They are wild and free
As they should be
And as they fade from sight
Into the lands beyond
Their plaintive howls
Chill and thrill my heart.

Tiny Lives

Under the overhanging banks
Where the wild spring waters flow,
Glow worms hang like party lanterns
Shedding their pale glow
Green, blue and red to make a
Miniature night sky
In the damp cavern,
Here tiny creatures are dancing
In this secret place
A tiny symphony of voices,
Celebrating the Joy
Of their tiny lives.

Emergency Department

I'm at the E D again
Waiting to know what the problem is
I hope it is something simple
Easy to fix
I can't think of anything bad
To happen
I want this to be over.
I want the healers to help
They say this will be okay.
But maybe it won't.
It kills me to see her in pain
Don't want it to happen again.

Feeling Sad

Feeling sad
The situation bad
And you can't
Find a way out
Of this—

Keep believing
Keep positive
You will get
Through this.

Winter's chill embrace

After winter's chill embrace
Comes the first glimmers of hope
The tiny bud of green

Many days the cold blast of winter
Has frozen hope in our hearts
Bitterness of the cold
Sadness of dark days.
Long shadows fall across my heart.

Today the tiniest ray of hope
Shone in the darkness,
Flickering, growing stronger
Brighter till it has become
A flame of hope
And brightness of joy
My heart is reborn and
Full of hope and joy.
Life has returned.

Hope

Live with hope in your Heart
Leave room in your soul for believing
And one day
Heaven and Earth
Will be in harmony
Then the impossible
Will happen for you
Opportunities will appear
Where you thought there were none
So live with Hope in your Heart.

www.ingramcontent.com/pod-product-compliance
Lightning Source LLC
Chambersburg PA
CBHW040939030426

42335CB00006B/196